BOSTON

Belmont
Sommerville
Everett
Chelsea
Mystic River
Charlestown
Winthrop
Watertown
Cambridge
East Boston
West End
North End
Logan International Airport
Boston inner Harbor
Charles River
Beacon Hill
Down-town
Charles River Basin
Back Bay
Bay Village
Chinatown/ Leather District
Allston/Brighton
Fenway/ Kenmore
South End
South Boston
Boston Harbor
Chestnut Hill Res.
Newton
Mission Hill
Brookline
BOSTON
Old Harbor
Spectacle Island
Long Island
Jamaica Pond
Roxbury
Thompson Island
Jamaica Plain
Rainsford I.
Moon I.
Dorchester
Quincy Bay
Roslindale
Cow Island Pond
West Roxbury
Mattapan
Neponset R.
Charles River
Hyde Park
Quincy
Dedham
Milton
Braintree
93
90

BOSTON

THE CRADLE OF LIBERTY

Jacqueline Hope Raynor

Firefly Books

A Firefly Book

Published by Firefly Books Ltd. 2025

First Printing

Library of Congress Control Number: 2025933809

Library and Archives Canada Cataloguing in Publication
Title: Boston : the cradle of liberty / Jacqueline Hope Raynor.
Names: Raynor, Jacqueline Hope, author.
Description: Includes index.
Identifiers: Canadiana 20250165791 | ISBN 9780228105640 (hardcover)
Subjects: LCSH: Boston (Mass.)—Guidebooks. | LCSH: Boston (Mass.)—Description and travel. | LCGFT: Guidebooks.
Classification: LCC F73.18 .R39 2025 | DDC 917.44/610444—dc23

Published in Canada by
Firefly Books Ltd.
50 Staples Avenue, Unit 1
Richmond Hill, Ontario
L4B 0A7

Published in the United States by
Firefly Books (U.S.) Inc.
P.O. Box 1338, Ellicott Station
Buffalo, New York
14205

Cover and interior design: Jacqueline Hope Raynor
Photo Editor: Cathy Hoshino

Printed in China | DC

FSC www.fsc.org
MIX
Paper | Supporting responsible forestry
FSC® C188448

INTRODUCTION

Boston is a city that blends history, innovation, and character like no other. Known as a city of firsts, it introduced the country's first public park, first post office, and first public library. Harvard, the nation's oldest university and alma mater to eight U.S. presidents, calls Boston home.

Founded in 1630 by Puritan settlers, Boston became the cradle of the American Revolution. Its cobblestone streets and colonial architecture still whisper the stories of rebellion, courage, and change. Unlike many historic cities, Boston's landmarks are the real thing; not reconstructions but structures preserved in place. Walk the Freedom Trail and you'll pass 16 historic sites that trace the bold steps of revolutionaries fighting for independence in places where key moments in American history happened.

But Boston doesn't live in the past. Today, it pulses with energy as a global center of learning, research, and culture. Its world-class universities, cutting-edge hospitals, and innovative tech labs make it one of the most advanced cities on Earth. Step outside a lecture hall or lab and you'll find yourself in a thriving neighborhood filled with cozy cafés, eclectic shops, waterfront paths, and some of the best food in the Northeast.

For sports lovers, few experiences compare to a game at Fenway, where the roar of the crowd and the crack of the bat echo across generations. But the real magic of Boston is its unique blend of grit and grace: its proud neighborhoods, passionate locals, and streets where history and progress walk side by side.

From its stately colonial homes to its sleek skyline, Boston is a city of contrasts and connections; a place where the American story began and where it continues to be rewritten every day. We hope you'll enjoy your journey as you travel the pages of *Boston: The Cradle of Liberty.*

The ruins of Fort Warren stand on Georges Island, located just a brief boat ride from Boston's city center. Built to protect the city and completed in the early 1860s, Fort Warren was used as a training facility for Union soldiers during the Civil War. Georges Island is one of 34 islands and peninsulas within the Boston Harbor Islands National and State Park.

(Opposite) America's oldest lighthouse, Boston Light, sits on Little Brewster Island. Its light can be seen 27 miles into the Atlantic and it is the only lighthouse still actively staffed by the United States Coast Guard.

(Previous page) The dramatic Boston skyline at dawn.

These bronze statues of a mother duck and her babies are based on the popular book *Make Way for Ducklings*. Published in 1941, the perennial bestseller tells the story of a pair of mallard ducks who decide to nest and raise a family on an island in the lagoon at the Boston Public Garden.

(Opposite) The 24-acre Boston Public Garden, designed in the English style, is both smaller and more formal than its neighbor, Boston Common. In addition to its various monuments, the garden features an artificial lagoon and ornamental bridge. Since the 1870s, swan boats have glided over the waters to the delight of locals and tourists.

(Previous page) Boston Common is the oldest park in the United States. Once the setting of public hangings, more recently the 50-acre oasis has been the site of large outdoor concerts and many important speeches, including those by Martin Luther King Jr. and Pope John Paul II. The Common is part of the "Emerald Necklace" of parks and parkways that extend from the Common south to Franklin Park in Jamaica Plain, then Roxbury and Dorchester.

The Embrace, a 20-foot-tall bronze sculpture honoring Dr. Martin Luther King Jr. and his wife Coretta Scott King, and the 1965 Freedom Plaza where it stands were both unveiled on January 13, 2023. The date was chosen to coincide with Martin Luther King Jr. Day which falls on the third Monday of January. The Plaza also honors 69 civil rights and social justice leaders active in Greater Boston from 1950–1975.

(Opposite) Massachusetts State House is perched proudly upon Beacon Hill. The building, designed by architect Charles Bulfinch, was completed in January 1798 and served as a model for the U.S. Capitol Building in Washington. Its famous dome, sheathed in copper and brilliant gold leaf, is one of Boston's most cherished landmarks.

The *Bunker Hill Monument*, dedicated in 1843, stands beside the bronze statue of Colonel William Prescott, the leader of the colonial forces at the Battle of Bunker Hill. The granite obelisk commemorates the battle (June 17, 1775), one of the first major battles between the American Colonies and the British in the American War of Independence.

This 10-foot-tall bronze statue of Harriet Tubman is dedicated to the memory of the famous abolitionist, Underground Railroad conductor, spy, nurse, and women's rights crusader. The *Harriet Tubman Memorial*, also known as *Step on Board*, is located in Harriet Tubman Park in the South End neighborhood of Boston.

Frogs in Common is a series of bronze sculptures created by David Phillips that were unveiled in 2002 at Boston Common, between the Frog Pond and Tadpole Playground. These frogs are depicted doing various human activities complete with human names and personalities. Tommy is fishing while Angela is lost in thought.

(Opposite) The Longfellow Bridge over the Charles River is one of the most architecturally distinguished river crossings in the city. It was completed in 1907 and was known as the Cambridge Bridge until 1927 when it was renamed in honor of the poet and longtime Boston resident Henry Wadsworth Longfellow. The bridge carries Massachusetts Route 3, the MBTA Red Line, bicycle, and pedestrian traffic. Its two distinctive granite towers with their pointed tops have given it the nickname "the Salt and Pepper Bridge."

Cast in bronze by Thomas Ball and dedicated on July 3, 1869, this triumphant statue of George Washington on horseback is widely considered one of the finest in the city. It stands among the lush surroundings of the Boston Public Garden.

(Opposite) The top of the Boston Custom House Tower is one of the most distinctive features of Boston's skyline and blends classical architectural elements with dramatic vertical scale. The 496-feet-tall tower was added in 1915 to the original 1847 building. Near the top, on all four sides, are large illuminated clock faces which can be seen from much of the city. Above the clocks is a colonnaded observation deck topped with a steep pyramidal roof.

The Boston Marathon attracts more than 500,000 spectators each year, making it New England's most widely attended sporting event. It is the world's oldest annual marathon and ranks as one of the most prestigious events in the city. It is traditionally held on Patriots' Day, the third Monday of April. The first race in 1897 attracted just 15 participants; there are now an average of 30,000 registered participants each year. The event was inspired by the success of the marathon competition in the 1896 Summer Olympics.

(Opposite) The 60-story, 790-feet John Hancock Tower is one of Boston's most recognizable landmarks and towers over the surrounding buildings. It was completed in 1976 and remains New England's tallest skyscraper.

In 1928, President Calvin Coolidge flipped a switch at the White House and turned on the lights at the original Boston Garden for the first time. The Garden is famous in hockey and basketball circles as the home of the Boston Bruins and the Boston Celtics, but the inaugural event was a boxing match where local hero, "Honeyboy" Finnegan, triumphed over André Routis on November 17, 1928. The aging structure was replaced in 1995 and the new building is called TD Garden. The arena continues to host the Bruins and Celtics as well as music's biggest stars.

TD GARDEN
BRUINS
100
1924
2024
CENTENNIAL
BOSTON

The Boston Tea Party was an American political protest in defiance of the British government's taxation policies. On December 16, 1773, demonstrators boarded British ships and threw chests of tea into Boston Harbor. The protest was a pivotal event in promoting colonial support for the American Revolution.

(Opposite) The iconic Boston Wharf Company sign at 263 Congress Street, at the corner of Sleeper Street, is part of the historic industrial waterfront skyline of Boston. The industrial real estate company played a crucial role in the development of the city; during the 19th century the company built wharves and docks to accommodate the increasing maritime traffic; in the 20th century, as needs changed, many of the old wharf properties were converted into warehouses, factories, and commercial buildings. As the 21st century progresses, residential towers, office buildings, and hotels are appearing.

BOSTON WHARF CO.
INDUSTRIAL
REAL ESTATE

Located on the historic waterfront, Boston Fish Pier is a bustling hub for fishing boats, seafood markets, and delicious dining options. Unsurprisingly, this historic area is a favorite among locals and tourists alike. In the 1920s the pier was home to one of the largest fishing fleets in the eastern United States, processing 250 million pounds of fish per year at its peak. The pier and its associated buildings were listed on the National Register of Historic Places in 2017.

The Boston Convention and Exhibition Center, a massive 516,000-square-foot facility, was completed in 2004 as part of a major effort to rejuvenate the Seaport District. The site was home to the city's wool industry until the 1950s. Today, new high-rise hotels, luxury condos, and a subway line, along with the dramatic convention center, have been part of the area's urban renewal.

(Opposite) The Boston Children's Museum, founded in 1913 by teachers in the Jamaica Plain neighborhood, moved to its current location, a former wool warehouse on Fort Point Channel, in 1979. The museum's exhibits, many of which are designed to be interactive and educational, are part of a collection which includes over 50,000 objects.

DREN'S MUSEUM
Hoo
KITCHEN

Boston is known as a city of neighborhoods. Charlestown, with its colonial architecture, was one of the earliest settlements before being annexed by Boston in 1874. Because of their historic charm and proximity to downtown, both Charlestown (opposite) and Beacon Hill (above) are considered highly desirable residential areas. Cobblestoned Acorn Street (above), built in the 1820s, is typical of the Beacon Hill neighborhood, known for its Federal-style rowhouses, gas street lanterns, and brick sidewalks. In addition to historic homes, the Massachusetts State House, Suffolk University, and Park Street Church are all found in Beacon Hill.

Founded in 1848, the Boston Public Library was the first large free municipal library in the United States. The large Italianate palazzo-style building on Copley Square, with the proud words "Free to All" emblazoned above the entrance doors, opened in 1895. Its many architectural features include the soaring 50-foot barrel vault ceiling of Bates Hall (opposite), the original reading room at the Central Library. Much of the room is original, including the tables and bookcases. Other features have been restored to match their original appearance, such as the signature green lamps.

EXIT

The Steaming Kettle on Sears Crescent has been a Boston landmark since 1873, when it was hung over the door of the Oriental Tea Company on Court Street. A city of immigrants, many Bostonians didn't read or speak English when they first arrived, so representative signage like this teapot told shoppers exactly what could be found inside the stores.

(Opposite) The glassed-in lobby of Government Center MBTA Station lights up City Hall Plaza. When it opened in 1968, City Hall was a controversial and prominent example of Brutalist architecture, part of the modernist movement. In 2025 the building was designated a Boston Landmark and continues to generate controversy.

SAMUEL ADAMS
1722—1803
A PATRIOT
HE ORGANIZED THE REVOLUTION
AND SIGNED THE
DECLARATION OF INDEPENDENCE

The Hatch Shell, officially known as the Edward A. Hatch Memorial Shell, is an outdoor concert venue on the Charles River Esplanade in the Back Bay area of Boston. Built in 1939–1940, it is best known for hosting the Boston Pops annual Fourth of July celebration as well as free concerts and picnics during the summer months.

(Opposite) Faneuil Hall has functioned both as a town meeting place and a public market since its wealthiest merchant, Peter Faneuil, donated the land to the city of Boston in 1742. The Georgian red brick landmark has provided a platform for many of the nation's greatest orators. It was here that colonists first protested the *Sugar Act* of 1764, and coined the battle cry "no taxation without representation."

Boston's Financial District dominates the skyline seen from across the Charles River. Although it has no official boundaries or status, the Financial District is generally agreed to be bounded by Atlantic Avenue, State Street, and Devonshire Street.

(Opposite) The slender column of the Custom House Tower still dominates Boston's Financial District at dusk. Once located in almost every major seaport but now often a historical anachronism, custom houses were occupied by city officials who managed the paperwork and collected the duties for the import and export of goods.

The John F. Kennedy Presidential Library and Museum is located in a 10-acre park on Columbia Point. It overlooks the sea that JFK loved and the city that helped launch his political career. The soaring white concrete and glass structure was designed by I.M. Pei and officially dedicated in 1979.

(Opposite) The dramatic 115-foot wall of glass provides spectacular views from inside the John F. Kennedy Presidential Library and Museum. The library boasts numerous exhibits, including an extensive chronicle of the 1,000 days of Kennedy's presidency and the great issues, including the Cuban Missile Crisis and the Space Race, that faced the nation during that time.

FENWAY PARK
HOME OF THE
BOSTON
RED SOX
THE
521
OVERLOOK
FENWAY PARK
ON AIR
WEEI
ON AIR
FENWAY PARK
GATE
C
BLEACHER BAR

Fenway Park is home to the Boston Red Sox. One of the American League's eight charter franchises, the club was founded in 1901. The team has won nine World Series championships and has played in 13 World Series but has had one of the longest championship droughts in history; after 1918, they didn't win the World Series again until 2004. This winless streak has been called the "Curse of the Bambino" because their star player Babe Ruth was sold to the rival New York Yankees in 1920.

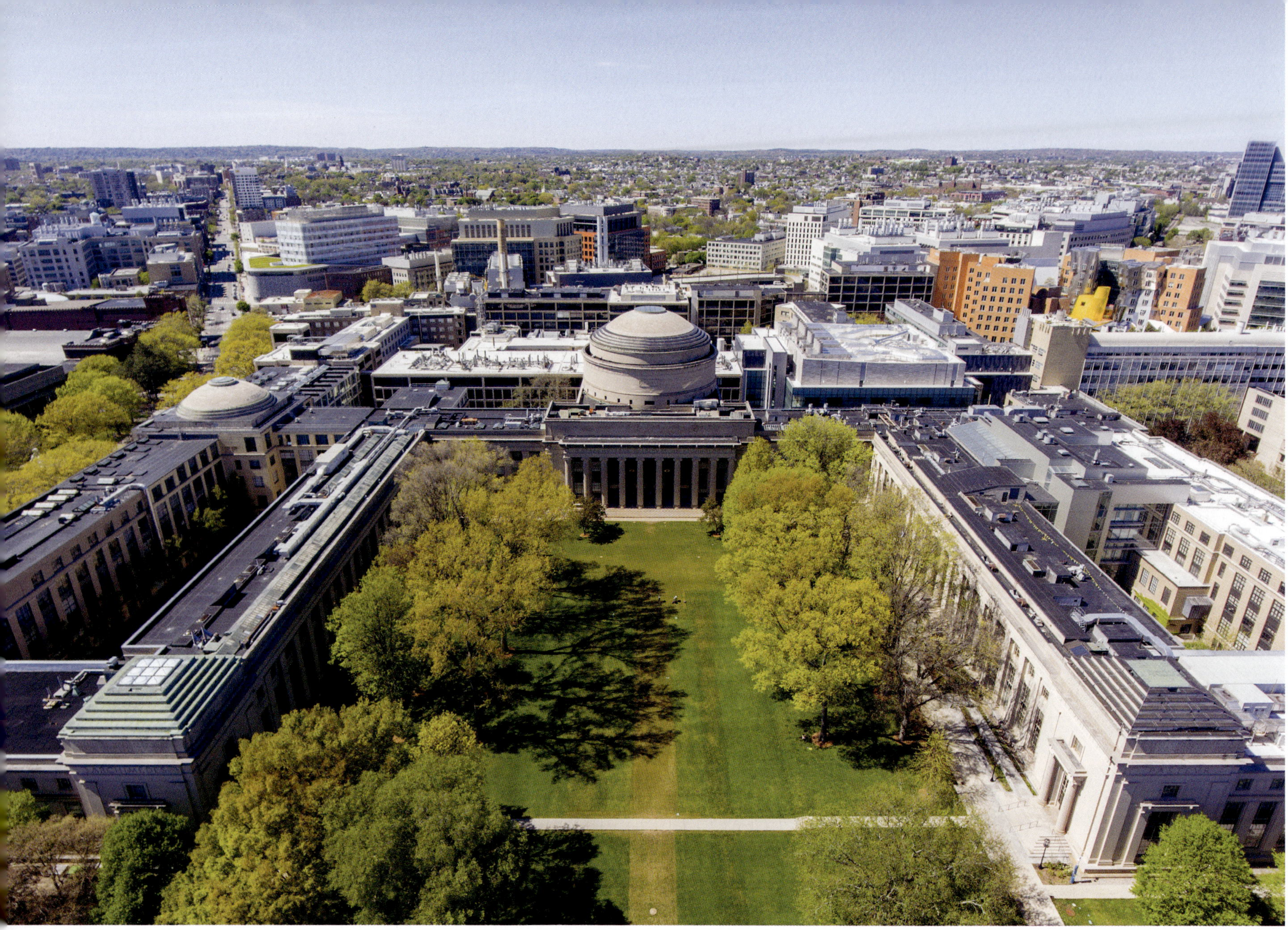

The Massachusetts Institute of Technology in Cambridge, founded in 1861, has evolved over the years to become one of the foremost universities in the world for the study science and engineering. Several architectural masterpieces dot the MIT campus.

(Opposite) The Ray and Maria Stata Center for Computer, Information and Intelligence Sciences (usually referred to as the Stata Center) was built on the site of MIT's legendary Building 20, a temporary timber-framed building constructed during World War II. Frank Gehry's glorious 430,000-square-foot academic complex, opened in 2004, paid tribute to the original building's ramshackle design and challenged the conventional design ideas of how laboratories and offices should look and function.

In 2010, *The Alchemist*, a stainless steel sculpture by Jaume Plensa, was installed in front of the Stratton Student Center, MIT. The hollow figure is composed of numerals and mathematical symbols to honor MIT's traditional STEM-focused teaching and research.

(Opposite) Boston's Institute of Contemporary Art moved to this stunning steel, glass, and wood building on Fan Pier in 2006. Unveiled to critical acclaim, it is the first new art museum to open in the city in nearly 100 years.

The Commandant's House, with panoramic views of Boston Harbor, is one of the oldest structures in the Charlestown Navy Yard. Since the Yard was decommissioned in 1974, the Commandant's House has been preserved by the National Park Service as part of Boston National Historical Park.

(Opposite) Launched in 1797, the USS *Constitution*, affectionately called "Old Ironsides," is the oldest American commissioned naval warship still afloat. Noted for her service during the War of 1812, she served as a training ship during the American Civil War and was only retired from active service in 1881. Designated a museum ship in 1907, she continues to have a full crew of 75 officers and sailors and participates in ceremonies and education programs while continuing to be open to visitors year-round. The *Constitution* is usually berthed at Pier 1 of the former Charlestown Naval Yard.

USS CONSTITUTION

Harvard University is rich in history. Puritan leaders in the Massachusetts Bay Colony established a college here in 1636; two years later, John Harvard died and bequeathed not only his books but also half his estate to the young school, which was subsequently named after him. As well as being the oldest university in the country, Harvard is one of the most prestigious schools in the world. Founded in 1782, Harvard Medical School, housed in Gordon Hall (above), is one of the oldest and most prestigious medical schools in the United States.

The John W. Weeks Bridge, a pedestrian bridge over the Charles River, was built in 1927. It connects Harvard University's historic Cambridge campus with its expanding Allston campus, home to facilities such as the Harvard Business School and newer academic buildings. The Weeks Bridge is a popular spot from which to observe the Head of the Charles Regatta. The world's largest 3-day rowing competition, it attracts over 300,000 spectators and 11,000 competitors.

This famous statue of Edgar Allan Poe, called *Poe Returning to Boston*, is located at Edgar Allan Poe Square. In dramatic fashion, the poet is accompanied by the eponymous bird from his famous 1845 poem "The Raven."

(Opposite) Boston has had multiple aquariums since the 1880s. This current incarnation, the New England Aquarium, opened in 1969 and continues to evolve as exhibits are added and expanded. A principal attraction of the aquarium is the Giant Ocean Tank where Myrtle, the green sea turtle, took up residence in 1970 and can still be visited today. For more than 50 years the Aquarium has provided innovative education and programming aimed at protecting the ocean and the creatures living in it.

PROTECTING THE
BLUE PLANET
Café
Gifts
Thanks for visiting!

Boston's Museum of Fine Arts is one of the largest fine arts museum in the United States. It contains nearly half a million treasures that range from Egyptian mummies to works by Monet, Rembrandt, van Gogh, and Renoir. (Opposite) Cyrus Edwin Dallin's *Appeal to the Great Spirit* stands at the entrance.

The Museum of Science, located in Science Park, is situated atop what was once a flood control dam at the mouth of the Charles River. Since its establishment at this site in 1951, the museum has expanded to include theaters, a planetarium, and a wide array of exhibits. Today, it boasts more than 700 interactive displays that engage visitors in science, technology, and engineering.

(Opposite) Now dwarfed by skyscrapers, the old State House was the seat of the colonial government for more than 60 years during the 18th century and is as the oldest surviving public building in Boston. Within these walls, Samuel Adams, James Otis, John Hancock, and John Adams debated the colony's future. From the balcony, the Declaration of Independence was read to Bostonians in 1776. Over the years the building has been used in many ways, including as Boston City Hall, a Masonic lodge, and a produce market.

CONGRESS

East Boston was known as Noddle Island for more than two centuries, named in honor of William Noddle, who first settled in the area around 1630. The old name is remembered at the pavilion in Piers Park, a six-acre park that reclaimed a condemned industrial pier, allowing residents and visitors direct access to the waterfront for recreational use.

The Prudential Center complex boasts two of the most recognizable buildings in Boston. The Prudential Tower, colloquially known as the Pru, was completed in 1964 and is one of the tallest buildings in the city. Including its radio mast, the tower's pinnacle height reaches 907 feet. 111 Huntington Avenue (viewed to the left of the Prudential Center) opened in 2002. Although only 554 feet tall, it's unique dome gives the tower the unofficial nicknames The R2-D2 Building and the Juicer Building.

Boston's Little Italy, known to locals simply as the North End, is the city's oldest residential community; it has been continuously inhabited since the city was founded in the 1630s. Although less than half-a-square-mile in area, the neighborhood has dozens of restaurants and tourist attractions and is one of the most popular destinations in the city.

(Opposite) The Christopher Columbus Waterfront Park, in the North End of Boston, decorated for the season.

OLD CITY HALL
45

Named after the granary that stood here in colonial days, the old Granary Burying Ground opened in 1660. Today, hardly any stones mark actual burial spots – the orderly arrangement is a result of grounds-keeping efforts. The Granary Burying Ground is the final resting place of many Revolutionary War heroes, including Paul Revere and three signers of the Declaration of Independence: John Hancock, Samuel Adams, and Robert Treat Paine.

(Opposite) Boston's Old City Hall served as the center of government for more than a century, from 1865 to 1969. Now occupied by offices and a restaurant, this grand structure is one of the earliest examples of adaptive use in Boston. In the 1960s, the trend was to tear down old buildings rather than reinvent them.

Rising amid Boston's skyscrapers, Park Street Church has held one of the city's most influential pulpits since 1809. The building's design was adopted from one by English architect Sir Christopher Wren and features a 217-foot white-painted steeple. The American militia stored gunpowder in the basement of the church during the War of 1812.

(Opposite) This grand Romanesque structure is part of the world headquarters of the First Church of Christ, Scientist, which occupies a 14-acre site at the corner of Huntington and Massachusetts Avenues. The original church was built in 1894; since then, there have been several additions including a library, reflecting pool, and fountain.

SCHOOL
SPEED
LIMIT
20

This stained-glass window in Boston's Massachusetts State House commemorates the Magna Carta as a foundational influence on the American Constitution.

(Opposite) Revolutionary War reenactments and living history events are popular throughout Boston and surrounding areas, particularly around Patriots' Day, commemorating the start of the war.

When the Big Dig buried a major stretch of Interstate 93 beneath downtown Boston, it freed up valuable urban land once dominated by traffic. The city transformed this reclaimed space into gardens, plazas, and tree-lined promenades across several neighborhoods. The most prominent of these is the Rose Fitzgerald Kennedy Greenway — a ribbon of four connected parks that trace the old highway route, offering Bostonians a vibrant and much-needed escape where congestion once reigned. The Big Dig, which included the construction of the Leonard P. Zakim Bunker Hill Bridge, was the most expensive highway project in American history. Originally slated for completion in 1998 at a cost of $7.4 billion, it was finished in December 2007 at a final cost exceeding $21.5 billion.

(Following page) The Zakim Bridge is a cable-stayed bridge in a harp configuration with cradles carrying each strand through their pylon. The main portion of the bridge carries four lanes each way and two additional lanes are cantilevered outside the cables, carrying more northbound traffic. The bridge, opened in 2003, has improved the flow of traffic in Boston immeasurably.

The *Equestrian Statue of Paul Revere* was completed in 1940. While the sculpture was first modeled in clay in 1885 by Cyrus Edwin Dallin, the casting in bronze and subsequent dedication took place nearly 55 years later.

(Opposite) Paul Revere owned this small clapboard frame house, the oldest surviving example in the city, from 1770 to 1800. It was from here that the Revolutionary War hero began his famous "midnight ride." Purchased in 1902 by the patriot's great grandson, the house was saved from demolition and opened its doors to the public six years later.

Arthur Fiedler, Conductor of the Boston Pops, was honored in 1984 with this statue near the Charles River Esplanade. Over the course of his fifty-year leadership the Pops became one of the most popular orchestras in the United States.

(Opposite) Symphony Hall opened in 1900, replacing the Old Boston Music Hall as the home of the Boston Symphony Orchestra. It also became the home of the Boston Pops and is widely considered one of the finest concert halls in the world — and the best in the United States. The hall features one of the world's premier concert organs, installed in 1949. When the original stage floor had to be replaced in 2006, great care was taken to preserve the hall's renowned acoustics: the new floor was painstakingly crafted using the same materials and construction techniques as the original.

BOSTON POPS
Fidelity
BOSTON POPS

PARK
THE FIRST SUBWAY
No
1752

Opened in 1897, the Green Line is Boston's oldest subway line, operating as a light rail and streetcar system. It runs underground through the downtown core and emerges to street level in the surrounding neighborhoods.

(Opposite) A mosaic mural on the walls of the Boston T Green Line notes the line is the first subway built in the United States.

(Following page) The elegant and historic skyline of Boston on a beautiful summer's day.

SALTY DOG
Seafood Grille
SALTY DOG
Oyster Bar
LifeWear

Built in the 1820s in the Greek Revival style, Quincy Market was designed to better accommodate the bustling trade surrounding Faneuil Hall. The market was later named after Boston Mayor Josiah Quincy. By the mid-20th century, the buildings had fallen into disrepair and faced demolition, but a dedicated group of citizens successfully petitioned in the 1970s to preserve and revitalize them. Today, Quincy Market remains a vibrant shopping and dining destination, drawing more than 18 million visitors each year.

(Following page) Originally part of the Charles River, the area now known as Back Bay was transformed through an extensive land reclamation project completed by 1880. This ambitious effort filled in the river with earth, creating space for a thriving and densely populated neighborhood. At its heart lies bustling Copley Square, home to Trinity Church, the Boston Public Library, cultural festivals, and farmers' markets. Elegant brownstones line the residential streets, while visitors stroll along Commonwealth Avenue to admire monuments honoring many of Boston's most celebrated citizens.

Unveiled in 1998, the *Irish Famine Memorial* honors the victims of the Irish Potato Famine (1845 to 1852). By 1850 some 35,000 Irish immigrants fleeing the famine had arrived in the city; today nearly one quarter of Boston's population is proud of its Irish heritage.

(Opposite) Trendy Newbury Street, in the Back Bay area, offers eight blocks of exclusive art galleries, designer boutiques, and restaurants.

UpWest
cattivo
RHONE
172 Newbury Street
RETAIL

Opened in 1903, the elegant Isabella Stewart Gardner Museum houses a remarkable collection of more than 7,500 works of art, including masterpieces by Titian, Rembrandt, Vermeer, and Sargent. Yet the museum is perhaps best known for being the site of what many consider the greatest art heist in history. In the early hours of March 18, 1990, thieves stole 13 paintings and sketches — valued at an estimated $500 million — including works by Rembrandt, Vermeer, Manet, and Degas. Despite a $10 million reward for information leading to their recovery, the case remains unsolved. Today, the empty frames of the stolen artworks still hang on the walls, serving as silent reminders of the loss.

天下為公
Pot Buffet
糕點

The Paramount Theater, in the heart of Boston's Washington Street Theater District, opened in 1932 as a 1,700-seat, single-screen movie theater. It was one of the first movie houses in Boston to show talking motion pictures. In 2005, Emerson College announced plans to renovate the theater and build a performing arts facility in and around the original building; the new Emerson Paramount Center officially opened in 2010, including a black box theater, the Bright Family Screening Room, a sound stage, and a scene/prop production shop.

(Opposite) Founded in the early 1800s, Boston's Chinatown is the oldest in the United States. Bordered by Boston Common and the Washington Street Theater District, it is also one of the most densely populated residential neighborhoods in the city. The official entrance to Chinatown — a decorative gate flanked by guardian lions — was built in 1982 as a gift from Taiwan to the city of Boston.

(Following page) The Boston Public Garden in the snow.

PUBLIC
GARDEN
1837

PHOTO CREDITS

ALAMY

Rainer Lesniewski: 2; dbtravel: 10–11; Peter Tsai Photography: 13; Washington Imaging: 16; Zuma Press, Inc.: 24; Terry Mathews: 28–29; Alan Myers: 30; Kenneth Grant: 34; Kenneth Grant: 36; Michael Dwyer: 39; Danita Delimont: 42; Jeremy Graham: 45; Sergi Reboredo: 49; Sergi Reboredo: 53; Michael Neelon: 56; Adam Eastland: 57; Alex Holder: 68; Dennis K. Johnson: 74; Iain Pritchard: 79; Melvyn Longhurst: 86; Glasshouse Images: 89; Jorge Garrido: 90

iSTOCK

Sean Pavone: 32; Marcio Silva: 33; APCortizasJr: 61; Dee: 66; f11photo: 67; Elijah-Lovkoff: 84–85

SHUTTERSTOCK

Gregory Bombard: 6–7; LouieLea: 8; Michael Sean Oleary: 9; Steven Noroian: 12; Heidi Besen: 14; Sean Pavone: 15; Heidi Besen: 17; Rosemarie Mosteller: 18; aphotostory: 19; Sean Pavone: 20; Jerry Gantar: 21; Marcio Jose Bastos Silva: 22; Galiptynutz: 23; TLF Images: 25; NayaDadara: 26; Wirestock Creators: 27; Marcio Jose Bastos Silva: 31; Hope Phillips: 35; quiggyt4: 37; Diego Grandi: 38; Wangkun Jia: 40; Sean Pavone: 41; Brett Welcher: 43; Marcio Jose Bastos Silva: 44; Wangkun Jia: 46; f11photo: 47; Wangkun Jia: 48; Millionstock: 50; Dominionart: 51; Jay Yuan: 52; NoyanYalcin: 54; Catrina Genovese: 55; Richard Cavalleri: 58; Marcio Jose Bastos Silva: 59; Michael 14: 60; Marcio Jose Bastos Silva: 62; eskystudio: 63; Wangkun Jia: 64; Jaclyn Vernace: 65; James Kirkikis: 69; Jaclyn Vernace: 71; Wangkun Jia: 72–73; AevanStock: 75; James Kirkikis: 76; VDB Photos: 77; Wangkun Jia: 78; ESB Professional: 80–81; 4kclips: 82; Paper Cat: 83; Marcio Jose Bastos Silva: 87; LnP images: 88; travelview: 91; Marcio Jose Bastos Silva: 92–93; ALEXANDRE F FAGUNDES: 96

WIKIMEDIA

Greenway Conservancy: 70

INDEX

The Democratic Donkey statue, installed in 1998 in the courtyard of Old City Hall, serves as a charming and interactive piece of public art, inviting visitors to engage with Boston's political history in a lighthearted manner.